'Ruby's book is full of lyrical archeology. She unearths words and feelings buried in the bones of our whakapapa. I don't know how you, a stranger to us, will read this book. I can only tell you how it is, as whānauka to consume these words like she has translated the braille of clay on rock from our tupuna.'
—Arihia Latham, *Kete*

'Extraordinary and powerful. A debut poetry collection that is full of movement and reflection.' —Vic Books Journal

'*Tōku Pāpā* is full of connection, especially with her hands and heart.' —Hamesh Wyatt, *Otago Daily Times*

Tōku Pāpā

RUBY SOLLY

TE HERENGA WAKA
UNIVERSITY PRESS

Te Herenga Waka University Press
PO Box 600 Wellington
New Zealand
teherengawakapress.co.nz

Te Herenga Waka University Press
is formerly Victoria University Press.

A catalogue record is available at the National Library of New Zealand.

ISBN 9781776564125

Published with the assistance of a grant from

ARTS COUNCIL OF NEW ZEALAND TOI AOTEAROA

Printed by Blue Star, Petone

All illustrations by Leisa Aumua.
p. 5: 'The embryo of the kiwi'
p. 11: 'Pūkeko'
p. 39: 'Diamond'
p. 80: 'Taura'

When you first told me
about *the white man*
I saw him as one great entity,
crushing villages with each step,
pushing chiefs to the ground
with his heavy tread.
Pulling entire species from the sea and land
only to crush them
between lake-sized fingerprints,
leaving only fossils.

When you first told me
that you believed
that even Pākehā should have
a little bit of Māori in them
to be counted as part of our world,
I asked if that applied to Mum.
You told me it did,
and that you'd always think of her
as an immigrant
even though her blood had circled here
for six generations
and counting.

When you first told me
that you gave me the name of our tupuna
so that I would be strong enough
to hold our family inside my ribcage,
I believed you.

Here you are.
Here is how I saw you,
trapped in your own amber.
Now it's time
for you to believe me.

Contents

Awe

Kura

awe

1 (noun) downy feathers, as on a baby bird or under an adult bird's wing.

2 (noun) the essence of the soul.

3 (noun) strength, power, influence.

How to Meet Your Future Husband in His Natural Habitat

You will find him
somewhere between the tallest tōtara,
and the deepest ocean.

Then he will press you,
hands first
into the moss beneath.

And as you fall,
you will hear the pūrerehua
summon the rains.

When they fall,
press your hands
further into his back.

Carve him new valleys,
sculpt mountain ranges from
his shoulders.

Exhale as you watch them
close the gap between sea
and sky.

White White Mistletoe

He tells you to put on your boots.
You leave the house and walk into the bush,
letting him find you doorways through dense walls of green.
He holds your hand and edges you over moss and wood,
bird calls overtaking the low scrape of small town traffic.

He looks to his wrist, reads veins as a river map,
helping you to cross as if the water is no more
than a sculpted line,
chiselled into the globe.

One of his tūpuna was a mapmaker.
The old uncle traversed the southern rivers
waiting for Beattie to show up on his bike;
pale hands eager to take
what could never be written down completely.

He knows this man,
even though he doesn't know about him.

A mist rolls up from the ground,
breathing out warm air
as he points above;
Tupeia Antarctica, white white mistletoe.

He kisses you like you are the only people alive right now.
Like this is Eden.
Like this is the old world.
Christmas has come early, he says.
Christmas has come at last.

Arrival

I have an aunty
who says she remembers
what it's like to be born.
She describes a feeling of warmth
and a blinding of light
like staring into the sun.

For many, it's hard to imagine a life before we exist.
But not for us who walk backwards into our futures.
The past getting smaller and smaller,
like being driven away from your first home,
looking behind you out the back window.
The trees waving you on to the cities,
where your family name is nothing but sounds
rolling around the mouth.

We believe the spirit is formed
when the eyes develop in utero.
Our two waters mingling
in a river encased with sinew and skin.
Ancient knowledge from a waka so sacred
that those aboard did not eat,
that the women were left behind
to weep on the beaches.
Piercing the sound barrier
with wails of sacrifice
for the greater good.

I know that Aunty was lying.
Before arrival
I remember a darkness,

like being underwater at night.
Then a sense of deep knowing,
and then fear.
Nothing but fear.

Whetū Hana

after 'Bright Star' by John Keats

My baby, my Whetū Hana, I wish I was as peaceful as you.

      Not unknowing, but innocent. Let me teach you to te reo o
      te marama

and I will watch you search for ghosts in her.

      Like nature's daughter, sleepless and illuminated.

The river echoes kā whetū, pulling them under and over.

      The smoke in my lungs echoes your breath in the air.

The falling snow echoes the shifting stars above us.

      Yes—you are my child, yet malleable still.

Pillow'd here on my warm chest. Your hands seeming to grow as I
hold them.

      Eyes trapping the night's mild lights.

Tonight we are awake, alone together. Trying to hold te marama
between our fingers.

      Still, still enough to hear her tell us how much it hurts to
      become.

And so, Whetū Hana, we'll live here for always, in the mists of her
breath.

Six Feet for a Single, Eight Feet for a Double

After the Kāi Tahu mōteatea 'Manu Tiria'

My father leaves school to dig graves.
The first break is the hardest.
The pressure of foot on steel,
the smell of earth rising.
Kōia kōia, e tau e kōia.
The men sit with packed lunches,
talking about the weather
next to holes they have dug themselves.

When he leaves the job, he keeps his shovel.
Always comes home to dig for the whānau.
Kōia kōia, e tau e kōia.
He keeps me playing graveside,
tells me off for climbing the pile of earth.
Sends me to find things;
the grave with the lamb,
the grave with the clasped hands.

He says this is how the dead speak.
A lamb for a child,
clasped hands pulling each other up to heaven;
but this is not the only way.
The atmosphere traps us in our bodies,
holds our teeth and tongues in place.

My father says he has no rhythm
but when he digs you see it in his body,
the flow through the earth into the feet, contracting the calves
through the spine, to chiselled arms,
through aging hands, into the shovel
and back into the whenua.

Kōia kōia, e tau e kōia.
With each beat he piles up dirt higher and higher,
making a lofty mountain
for us to bow to.

Missing

In the bush that surrounds our home
a child has gone missing.

Her parents told her to *go and look for kiwis*
    and off she went into the snow-dusted bush,
        past the signposted ways,
            past the chimney smoke's drift,
                past the river of ice and slumbering eels.
                    Off she went into our tapestry of flora and snow,
                        in sparkly sandals and a summer dress.

A man speaks on TV about a rescue mission
as helicopters ring overhead
filling the bush with the beats of pūrerehua,
tempting our southern rains.
His hair combed to one side as a slick wave,
uniform constellated with badges.

All the while, you are out there
strong and suffering,
following the maps in your head.
Scanning the landscape
for that flash of foreign plastic.
White skin, on dark moss.

He Manawa Mauka

We are dwarfed by a snow bank
that reaches beyond our eyes,
a single hole punctuating its white sheet.
Your hand covers my small eyes
and I feel you shielding me in the warmth of your jacket
as we move through.

I open them to a palace of ice and snow
meticulously carved by strangers
long gone down the mountain.

We sit together in silence,
deep in the mountain's quiet heart.
Watching our breath melt away
the walls around us.

Pup

From the helicopter
they see thousands of dots moving away from the mountain
as plumes of grey penetrate the air.

A river of ash maps a new landscape
as several dots negotiate their way towards
a chaos of magma and snow.

You see a car
third carpark down,
white Toyota.
A small Jack Russell inside.

You wrap your arm in a jersey and punch your way in.
The glass triggers a bite so forceful
that the snow is freckled with your blood.

The dog's teeth hold strong,
its fear pumping into your arm.

But you just take it,
let it circulate
through the body
let it dissipate in each cell.
All while the mountain thunders underneath you,
all while you hold him and say

> *It's ok, pup*
> *it's ok*

Better and Braver

In a place I've never been, my small hand is pressed in yours
as we walk a path lined with moulting trees.
You tell me you are teaching me how to be
better and braver.

I nod at you as the words sail over me,
puddle-stomping till the concrete vibrates under my feet.

You drop my hand
as I enter one final puddle,
falling further and further down
until I am swimming in a dark hidden place.

From my wet prison
I watch you above, mouthing
better and braver.

I wake in my bed to find I am smaller than myself
and burst further
and further into tears.

Makawe—Tuatahi

For Walter George Koha

You buried my whenua at a motel.
Under a palm tree, next to where the trucks go by.
I see myself watching you,
young, tanned and heaving
as dirt moves from under the ground
to over it.
Watching
as I soak into the soil
before being covered up to rest.

When my brother is born
you bury his on someone else's mountains,
under a five finger.
Hands always waving in the wind.
He is not there to see you cover him
with a blanket
of volcanic earth.

You cut a lock of my hair
and a lock of my mother's.
Place them in each tiny hand,
have the ends coil around
the sapling limbs.
The red fleck of my hair
catching in the light
as we hope silently
for his grip to
tighten.

Custard

When I was smaller than the family dog,
Dad would tell Mum
that he was taking me to kōhanga.
Then we'd go to the bakery
and get as many custard pies
as we could handle.

Park up by the river,
talk,
eat,
listen to the radio a while.

He'd light one up
as fat as the mighty brown trout,
captured and killed
and lull me to sleep
with a puku full of custard
in his red van
with all his windows up.

Now I am grown
and you ask me to explain something you said.
My eyes glaze
and all I can see is that
red van,
pastry flakes resting
in the corners of my sleeping mouth.

The Machete

You drive me three hours inland to see the national ballet.
You tell me it takes ten thousand hours to get onto the stage
and I feel the weight of ten thousand hours, pressing me
like a flower under a book
too difficult for me to read yet.

When we get home, through my window I watch you take your
    rusty machete.
Watch you press it to its grindstone,
see the push and pull of preparation bubbling under your skin.
Carving the air as you move towards the gorse and blackberry
invading your native Eden.

I fog the glass, tiptoe from my hiding place
towards the door as you close your eyes to feel the current of the air.
You lift me up and press my hand firmly into the handle,
my bare legs dangling above our tiny forest of black, yellow
    and green.
We conduct the air with the edge of your blade
your hand tightening around me with each cut you make.

It takes ten thousand hours to be an expert
and I quit ballet the following year.
You tell me that I can have my own machete at fifteen.
Pāpā, I am still waiting to inherit your blade.

Free Diving

He cradles an arm full of bottles,
lugs them to a car full of kids.
We sift through a sea
of bottle caps,
practise our flutter kick
through metal tides.

He lets me hold the wheel
while he opens one.
The car wavers
under guidance of miniature hands.

He pulls out a rope marked at each metre,
drops it into the water for us to chase.
Bring me some sand from the bottom, as proof.
The others swim down
but miss every time.
Always come back
red and gasping.

You've got to meditate on it, tāku kōtiro.
If you flip it all on its head,
turn the birds above you into fish,
you'll be able to swim in the sky below you.
You won't need to worry
about not being able to breathe.

I lie back, head tilted up
and let myself fall
into the sodden sky.

Driftwood

We're all just driftwood here, bub.
The storm has eaten
our landscape.
He and I
must map our new land.

He slips a lighter from his pocket,
holds it in his hand
as if it is an orphaned bird.

Some come here for the prison,
others because of the cost,
but no one stays here on purpose.

We are hunting
for the storm's gifts.
Carved driftwood
lines our new shore.
This is our consolation prize.

He lights up.
The flame in his hand
is painting the sky with
all the colours
we no longer have on land.

Makawe—Tuarua

By ten years old
my hair is nearly as long as me.
Each night I sit with my mother
for the silent ritual
of brush and braid.

When she leaves,
you are in charge.
Master of under and over.
As the lightbulb flickers
you tell me of a dream you have
where you are moving along a straight line
for a long, long time
and then you start to swerve.
Each time, this is where you wake.

You braid tight.
This rope is important,
our days are so short here
and you need it to pull back the sun.
You know how thick my skin is,
you know how much I can handle.

I feel your grip ebb away as we sit in our silence.
I turn to find you have come to the end,
and see your hands braiding
the air. Your eyes stare into
something ahead of me,
something that I can't yet see.

River Songs—Tauranga Taupō

You want me to be a strong swimmer
because girls who swim
can always get themselves out of trouble.

The other kids around here
get little boats for Christmas.
They take them down the river,
launch them from the mudflats.
Push and pull new oars
until they are only distant toys
to those on the shore.

But not me.
You take us all up the river,
drop us into the current.
The others in their little boats
or straddling old tyres.
But not me.
I need to learn how to swim.
Through rapids we go,
my legs weaving through debris.

When I was small,
you took me in your arms
and walked me out into the water for the first time.
I watched my mother on the shore
getting smaller and smaller,
but I never cried or screamed.
Only opened my eyes
wider and wider
as she changed from person

to shape
to colour,
as the water darkened
around your waist.

When I am thrashing through rapids,
sticks and stones
cut me a map of red rivers
as the boats lag behind me,
their hulls rippling
the blood in my wake.

I always escape the mouth
before they arrive.
Each time, there you are
calling to all the fishermen
that they don't need to worry about me.
She's a girl who can go with the current.
She's a girl who can swim.

Ruru

In the darkness
there is a soft weight
making cracks in the silence.
Breaths weakening the air
in the room we all sleep in.
You knock on the window
and we come out to meet you.
You open up the crook of your arm
to show her nestled beneath.
Eyes wider than the moon
that lights you both.

One of the boys touches her
and she bites.
But your hands trickle over her,
a fine rain in summer
the smell all warm and petrichor.
She lets my fingers
sift her feathers
as you walk us both home.

Her call creeps through my window
and into my dream.
I am someone else
a long time ago.
I wake in the dream to hear
koukou, koukou.
Then wake into myself and hear again
koukou, koukou.
We have a tupuna named after the morepork's cry.
I think of how she must have been born singing.

Of how she married a man sent here to fight her,
how they named their son after an even rarer bird.
Maybe she was born screaming.
We will never know now.

Each night when we drive up our street
your morepork is there waiting.
She swoops in the headlights,
traces the river lines
that make our roads.
Moves between the car and the moon,
trapped between new and old light.

We swerve into the driveway
as she turns on the wing.
We hear her calling low
koukou, koukou.
We wait for her to scream,
we wait for permission to panic.

Makawe—Tuatoru

They keep asking me
when I'm going to cut it.
The girls come at me with scissors.
The click click of blades
snuck into sleepovers.
Hair on the pillow in the morning,
fine moss on the forest floor.

Tiny trims.
Offcuts gathered up
in a jar on the bathroom window.
Ritualistic preservation,
museum pieces behind glass.

Pāpā, we never had a korowai
but I have grown one.
I can wear nothing but myself
if I choose to.
If my shoulders are back and down
it sits perfectly upon them.

Past my feet it grows
strangling me like a vine
from the ground up.
The birds return to nest in it,
weighing me down when they rest,
lifting me up when they soar.

The birds begin to braid
working in teams of three. I am a mass of ropes
pulling in all directions.

I can't remember what scissors are.
But I remember the sound,
I hear the click click in the wings.

The ropes reach and reach,
search for snow and salt
and the waters where they
touch. They will keep
growing until they can
reach
all the way home
and pull us back in.
My body trailing behind,
lifeless
in the water.

Pūkeko

Your sister tasks me
with collecting pūkeko feathers
from now until she dies
to fill her coffin.
On country roads she speeds
towards flashes of white and red.

Back home, you roam our wilderness
with food at the end of your hands
luring in your flock of blue.
Their long legs flexing and falling
in arcs behind you.
I watch from my window
as you bring them up to the glass.
They watch me with black eyes
and full mouths.
Your flock of fancy
in all the colours
of our modern nation.

In the aftermath
you are sleeping behind the sun
as the wind stirs feather and grass
into frenzies.
I follow your trail,
pluck feathers from the air,
shape my arms into wings.
I climb the tallest tree
and jump
hoping to fly
hoping to fall.

Eulogy

As a child
whenever I was angry,
inconsolable,
my father would tell me to write a eulogy
to the person who had caused me pain.
He said that by the end of it
I would see
that even those who cause us pain
are precious to the world.

> My father was an exceptional man,
> he was blessed
> with a gentle soul.
> He walked in step
> with the many animals he adored
> and he treaded lightly on this earth.

> He taught me
> to tread as he did
> and to leave the world as you found it.
> Ideally, improve it.

One day I will read this
to a room of faces I barely recognise.
I will look out on a world
no different with him gone
as it was
with him here.

kura

1 (noun) red feathers, feathers used as decoration, treasure, valued possession, heirloom, precious possession, sacred, divine law, philosophy, darling, chief.

2 (adjective) to be red, scarlet.

3 (noun) glow.

Te Whare o Hoani

On the first day,
Hoani pushed Rakinui
away from Papatūānuku
and let the light settle
like debris after a storm.
This will be our new land.

On the second day,
Hoani pulled trees from the ground.
Karakia echoed through his forests.
Rakinui wept rivers
onto volcanic sands.
A simple house is all we need,
easy to heat
and you always know
where all the tamariki are.

On the third day,
Hoani replenished the forest.
Soft earth gave way
to strong hands,
new roots burrowed down
towards the earth's inner heat.
When we take,
we give in turn.
It hurts to take,
but it hurt us all
to perish.

On the fourth day,
Hoani searched for food.

He pressed sunburnt ears to the ground
and he listened.
He lay on the forest floor
and the river bed
and he heard them breathing.
There is fish, fruit and water.
We will always be full
as long as we give back
what we take.

On the fifth day,
Hoani invited the animals
into his paradise.
The sky vibrated
with the migration of birds.
The ground shook
as all the animals ran in to meet him.
He stood in the centre of the land
arms raised, conducting them all.
We are all equal,
this will be home to us all.

On the sixth day,
Hoani provided for his whānau.
He fed them from the forest,
he fed them from the rivers,
and he kept them warm in his home.
The life from the land
flows into us all.
We nurture each other,
we leave no footprints.

On the seventh day,
and all the days thereafter,
Hoani rested
as the lands around him overgrew,
and the house in which he lived
was reclaimed by the land.
Let us build no fences
so that all the land we see is ours.

How to Pull a Trout from
the River With Your Bare Hands

First, you need to find
the perfect spot.
Trout are like people,
they like to hide.
Wade against the current.
This will be nothing new to you.
Look for the scales
shining back at you
like pounamu.

Then, turn yourself
so that you and your prey
are watching the same patch of sky.
Remember, as in all things,
your movements
must be gentle.

Now, dip your hand behind your fish.
Move it gently
until it is just under his belly.
Begin to move your fingers
in soft motions.
Slowly slide them up
until you feel his belly
resting against your fingers.

Patience is your greatest resource.
You need to stay with the fish
until he is completely entranced.

These will be his last moments.
Remember to respect his sacrifice.

Now, this is the hard part:
reach your other hand beyond the trout
and grab the tail
and throw the fish onto the shore.

Make sure to kill him humanely,
hit him on the head quickly.
No one wants to die
by drowning
in air.

Smoke

At eight years old
you walked into a smoke-filled garage looking for your neighbour.
Sadly you found him, already up in smoke.
You were the fastest at your school, you told me so it's true.
One time you ran around the whole lake while everyone else walked.
Smoked 'em you said. *Absolutely smoked 'em.*
Ran so fast that your shoes started smoking,
or was it steam up from the gravel road?
Who's to say, not me.

When you're halfway through the race, your brother drives past you
    in a ute,
offers you a lift to cut the corners.
But you keep running, that's how you smoked 'em all.
There's a picture of you in the local rag,
black and white,
playing rugby in sandshoes.
You're standing in place while boys in proper boots
are ready to mow you down.
You're steaming at the mouth—haka stance.
Player of the Day. Puts up a smokescreen yet again.

But where there's smoke there's fire, eh Pā?
It's good to be a funny boy though,
everybody loves the one who starts the fire at the party.
Playing shadow puppets
rude and juvenile
with shadows of the great stories.
This is a boy,
this is a car,
this is the smoke,
and this is its fire.

Cut

Cut scene to when I was born the second time,
seeing the way she showed me the cuts.
Telling her to cut it out inside my head.
But the words not cutting through my teeth.
I've got my work cut out for me now.
I've got my work cut out for me.

Cut my hair short the next chance I got,
became dressed low-cut, slim fit.
Cut my nails with my teeth.
Took a while for the government to cut in
and discover all the short cuts we'd taken;
they made us talk, cutting us off.
Trying to cut us apart, like hacking into the great fish.
Cutting out the middle man pulled us apart like white meat—
    not red this time.
We've got our work cut out for us now.
We've got our work cut out for us.

I tell you what happens and you cut me off with
I love you I love you I love you.
But never cut through to sorry.
Cutting the chord slowly, slowly.
Biting through it to cut my teeth in.
I've got my work cut out for me now.
I've got my work cut out for me.

Cut scene to present-day back country,
cutting the land with a knife as long as your arm.
We cut our conversation short.
Cut out the raruraru,

cut out the mamae,
cut through the earth
and bury them all deep
in the cuts we have created.
We've got our work cut out for us now.
We've got our work cut out for us.

Tīeke

It starts from the blur of opening your eyes in darkness.
It starts with the bush humming
the sound of water you cannot see.
An orange flicker moves through as a saddleback
comes centre frame.
Its red wattle hanging
as a sacred tear.

Then another comes, then another;
still more birds flood your landscape.

As the beat of wings rain down heavy,
you feel the pressure of a thousand tiny bones
weighing down your skin.

Still more birds come
as you feel the perimeters of open space
shrinking. Still, feathers
fight with sky
until there are more birds than bush
and you have no air
left to breathe.

Prey

You are standing on the dry grass,
arms out, eyes closed,
sun facing.

A single dove lands on your outstretched hand.
You do not react.
Another lands on the other.
You do not react.
More and more doves land across your frame,
the wings fuelling micro-currents
in the air they claim around your body.

A pack of dogs in a ute driving past
slice the silence
into small pieces that rain down around you.
You fall to your knees,
the doves scattering into the horizon

and then I know
why we are named after prey
and not predators.

Wairaki

Tuatahi

You told me once that water is just air but thicker
which taught me a lot about why I always feel
like I am on the verge of drowning.

Our tūpuna were good at drowning.
Straight off the boat at Gallipoli,
drowned before the battle began, seventeen and a half.

Another at Foxton Beach, trying to save a swimmer,
both losing in the process.

When you took me as a child to gather watercress,
holding my ankles and dangling my body in the water,
I started to enjoy the feeling of being taken.
Letting myself melt into the water.
Waiting until the last possible moment
to grab the prize
and signal to come up again.

You always told me not to swim there.
That a young uncle
had jumped into the heart of the falls.
That it drew the life from him
as it pushed him into the river mouth.

But the uncle wasn't yours.
He was Mum's, she said.
I guess when you love someone enough
their rivers become you.

As a child I thought that the shades of skin
came from coloured blood.
Our blood would get lighter
and lighter with each generation
until eventually my veins
would contain nothing
but water.

When cut for the first time, as if a great fish,
I saw nothing but red.
Ever since then I wanted to let it all out
until I was light enough to float on top of the water,
the skeletal structure of a sea vessel,
longing for someone to flesh me out.

But you were different,
wanting to keep those foreign tūpuna in you.
Feel them as jetsam in your rivers
that feed the dry earth.

When you love someone enough
you become the land they walk on.

I feel them all,
pulling me out of the water,
pushing air into my throat.
Against the current.
Against my will.

I imagine them all, swimming through you,
guests in their own homes,
weaving through the whakapapa
and knowing it's too dangerous
to break apart now.

Tuatoru

We were voyagers once you said
as we sat by a lake that was not our own.
Others wanted to be on the water,
but we have always wanted to be underneath it.

As a child, I encouraged a friend to swim without water wings
and then was the first to notice that they were drowning.
When I went in after them they climbed on my back,

like Paikea, pushing me closer towards the edge.
The feeling of panic dissipating as I felt something deep in me
move closer towards a home that I hadn't met yet.

Mum pulled me from the water and I felt it all.
Relief tainted with disappointment.
Shame rolling over me like a fever.

Now I voyage, searching for that feeling.
Staying under for too long, because I can.
Staying under for too long, because I can't.

I Dream You

For Nana

I go to see my grandmother and find her sleeping.
Her breath coming in stabs against the aircon.
Not alive, but not yet left us.
I was told once that some people are lucky enough to be brought up
while the rest of us are dragged there—
holding on to a rope underwater,
as those on the surface pull us towards them
and the blood in our ears pushes us inside out.

When I touch her arm
her eyes flicker open and closed.
She sees through me.
When her eyes open fully
she smiles and holds me.
I thought I dreamt you again . . .
Her grip tightening.
I dream you all the time . . .

I dream you too . . .
Skin to skin, in a white room again.
The family photos stacked in a drawer,
generation on generation.
All the time . . .
They breathe black and white
through the cracks in the wood.

She asks about the sea I have come from,
nods while looking beyond me
to a sky syrupy with clouds.
We could never get you out of the water when you were little,

always diving around eh, you'd be under so long we'd start to worry.
Under that wet film I was screaming
knowing that no one would hear me.
Then I'd return to the world
even more silent
than I was before I left.

Te Pukapuka a Hoani

{I am the bread of life}
If you are hungry, know that
the bush reaches up to the sky for you.
Taupō Moana is breathing with fish,
volcanic soil is heaving with rain,
and for you
all the rivers flow
into each other's arms.

{I am the good shepherd}
Do not be scared of the animals.
But speak to them
in their language,
touch them as gently as they touch you
and if you must kill them
do it with confidence
as to not cause them
a pain we cannot know.

{I am the resurrection and the life]
Tamaiti, everyone
believes in heaven
when they have seen death.

{I am the light of the world}
When the sun touches that tōtara,
I'll take you to the south to breathe
the same air as our people.
But we both know that the sun never hits there.
The sun is cruel to us both.

{I am the true vine}
People these days can turn
anything into a drug.
Light, sugar, money—
you're better off growing your own.
When you sit down to light up
and put the day to rest
at least you'll know
it's farm to paper.

{I am the gate for the sheep}
Please, come home to me
whenever you can.
There is a pot on the stove for tea.
Your room is the same
as you left it.
I am sorry
but the rest of our home
is filled
with old smoke.

{I am the way and the truth and the life}
When I die, wrap me in harakeke,
get your children
to kiss my cheeks,
bring the birds
to see me be still
and let them sing my soul
all the way
to the south.

River Songs—Waimāpihi

Pāpā, I've lived in this valley
ever since as falcons' prey
you dropped me in.

I hit the ground digging.
Sun piercing through
the cracks in the roadways.

This road runs deep here, Pāpā
and beneath it
the river deeper still.

I hear it rage under our atmosphere,
when I dream you
diving through concrete

with me holding your ankles.
They call this the Waimāpihi
after our tūpuna who bathed in these waters.

Ownership is different here,
it rises up from the ashes
of guardianship.

One night
I fall into her stream,
my body seizing

in an electric storm.
I feel her push up the concrete
that bars her from the sun.

Return to our valley, Pāpā.
You can have the bed,
I will weave a mat and sleep on the floor.

I will boil you potatoes and roots,
I will drink the broth.

I will pull the land up to meet you,
by pushing myself further and further into the sea.

You will walk a land as long as the eye sees,
while I rip down fences in your distance.

I will wrap you in blankets,
while I sleep pale and bare.

I will smash the concrete for you,
rise the river from the road.

You can run your hands over the valley,
trace the old riverbed.

Then I'll lay myself across it for you.
My hair becoming the watercress,

my bones the fish,
my blood the water,
my body the stony bed.

You can pile up
all of Wakefield's maps,
all of the deeds

and light them up.
Pāpā, we'll be ahi kā
once more.

Ōtautahi

1. We Are Different Kinds of Far Away

When it happens. When the bones in our urupā are shaken
and inch closer to where they come from.
I see you.

Central figure in a room populated with
books, boxes, bottles,
plastic rivers winding across your floor.

And I ask you
Did you feel anything?
Your voice cuts
I don't feel anything at all.

2. There Is a Woman with a Chip Implanted in Her Thigh

That allows her to feel every earthquake in the world.
I think of her as my feet search for sand in my cities,
for wind in my house,
for salt in my water.
I feel the earth pushing bones
up from the other side
as my bones push at my skin,
trying to sing themselves home.

3. Verbatim

The world has come to us, my girl.
That's why you feel this way.
We tried our best, we tried our best to protect you.
But you are not safe. We are not safe.
Blood has been shed on our whenua again.
Guns are the evil of all man.
And every word any one speaks
is a loaded gun.

Gold

I dreamt a woman
who was thinned from starvation.
Her teeth poking from her mouth,
her cheeks like deep caves in the silence.
Her hair pulling the wind inside it
as she sat on the beach I grew up on.

I turned and you were behind me.
She looked at you like I wasn't there.
Then she dove into the water
and swam towards the island.

I followed you home while you cried
into the dirt road, making pools behind you
that filled with flecks of gold.

When I awoke you borrowed a boat
and took me all the way to the island.
The island is really a peninsula, you told me.
You said it over and over: *peninsula, peninsula.*

We arrived to birds swarming a kōwhai tree
that protected the entrance to a cave.
Before we were here, these trees
marked beds for bones.
More and more birds came
as their circle widened to bring us in.

We did not go ashore.
These were not our old people.
These were not our birds.

At home, my mother is cooking,
my father is sleeping,
and I am hunting
for the yellow seeds on the earth.

I fill my hands. I feel myself scream
for a reason I can't find,
scattering birds
from the centre of our universe.

I am alone again,
standing here,
my feet covered in dirt,
my hands full of gold.

Out of the Blue

There's a knock at the back door.
I go out and there's this little kid,
about five or six, and a woman.
Skinny as, bleached blonde, leather jacket,
the works.
She's standing there rolling a tayli on my porch
while the kid looks me up and down,
eyes to boots, and goes
That's not him.

That's not who? I said,
and the woman goes
We're looking for the man with the gun.
She's still standing there,
face like a trout and she goes to me
Our cat's gone missing and we're gonna find who did it.

I told them I've never owned a gun.
I hate the bloody things.
Every evil on this land
can be traced back
to guns and men and greed.
For what it's worth, I hate cats too.
The birds round here?
They used to deafen you.
Now you've gotta listen hard
and wait for them to come.
Only man with a gun round here
is Johnny, and he's in it for rabbits,
for the meat, and to stop them chewing the ferns down.

So ya better get off my property, I said,
I didn't kill your cat.

Then the bloody woman
lights up on my porch
with that little kid right there breathing it in.
And she goes
You better not have done anything
or we'll be back.
Gets her ash everywhere, on my whenua,
takes her kid and walks off.
Did I really say all that?
Yeah of course I did.
Every last word.

River Songs—Te Puni (Influenza, 1918)

In the dream
the women are already dead.
They have been washed
into a river raging brown and blue.
They lie along its sides, like lilies
after a heavy rain.
All dark hair and pale skin,
like looking at myself
reflected in a mirror fogged
with someone else's breath.

The smell of burnt sugar
mixes with water and loam.
Vapours spreading like a sickness
in colours of mist and river spray.
The women are in white cloth
that rests gentle on the skin.
Water vapor pressing
wherever bones jut.
Shoulder blades, ribs,
the most angular points of the hips.

This is a soundless space,
before the sounds are born.
The kōauau calling the gods back in,
the porotiti pulling sickness from flesh,
singing a darker world into being.
The trees let leaves fall.
The birds moult feathers.
There is no one here
to see the difference

between stem and spine.
I wake to two new worlds.
Past and present compressed
into each cell,
unwinding in me
fraying out like a rope.

Kā Manu Ika

Today the trees are a violent sea.
Pulled and pushed
by Tāwhirimātea's invisible hands.

Fish out of water
hide in their nests today,
their offcuts sailing
through his fingers.

When I was smaller
than a light breeze,
I couldn't sleep at Nana's
because the cars were louder
than my dreams.

Then Pāpā taught me
to imagine each passing car
as a wave
crashing on our shore.

Today I sit here
and watch the tide
wash the birds back in.

Relations

When I was a baby
Pāpā took me out into the snow
to look at how it was lit by the moon.
According to family legend
I've been obsessed with white things ever since.

Daisies,
          puawhanaka,
sheets,
          cupcakes garnished with vanilla icing,
swans
on ponds the colour of my father's skin.
Bruised from generations of side-stepping
and running in bare feet.

White is always the middle of the flag.
The needle through which the black and the red entwine,
the exposure needed
to make the dark make sense.

When I go to my grandmother's
she bakes me stodgy bread
to plug the holes in me,
fills the gaps with golden syrup
and promises a new pat of butter
when the money goes in on Thursday.

When I take you to my history,
when I stand you on this earth and fill the gaps in you,
you must do more than clasp my hands behind your neck,
show your friends my developing patina
and hide me under your formal dress.

I hope you learn how my diacritics sound in person.
I hope that you can shoot arrows from my arms
into the battlefield
with its sides more like spectrums.

Oral Language Written Down

The stats say that neither you nor I read.
But Pāpā, our houses are lined with books.
Walls thick with paper, pulp and pine.
Breathing with the drought and damp of the seasons.

In winter we sit fireside,
watching your finger navigate the page.
Letters scattering like lizards
heading back to the underworld.

Stories are always the same.
It's us that changes.
Like how we dive into black pools
at night, to find each other

in the kitchen, reading
with the lights off,
watching the world
with the volume down.

Pāpā, you are dog-eared and brittle,
finger-printed and water-damaged.
While how I know you blooms
as ribs off a central spine.

Kei Hea Tōku Pāpā?

Dad, last night
I lost you again.
I dreamt us a beach
under a full moon reflected.

Your hands were moulding
a fallen tōtara.
Your fingers pulling away bark
and gliding through wood
as if it were no harder
than kamokamo.

I sat in the hollow
you had created for my body
and you pushed us out into the water.

In silence, you paddled behind me
and slowly your end of our waka
sank further into the water
until you were trapped
below its surface.
Your black eyes punctuating
the water between us.

I watched you slip further
and further down
until you were nothing but ripples,
until there was nothing around me
but the sea, and it was as if
you'd never even existed at all.

Small Animals

I once killed a mouse
by holding it too tightly.
The red from its eyes
faded to pink as it went limp
and then hard
like a cold statue of itself.

You showed me then
how to cup my hands
like a small globe.
Keeping a space
for an air-filled core to form
for a small animal
to coil itself in.

No matter how many times you showed me
I would tighten my fingers
so that each insect, each animal
was pressed against my hands.
Squirming more and more
as I tried harder and harder
to control it.

Children run to you to see the creatures
held gently in your hands
weaving themselves through fingers
that barely touch them.

My hands would clench so tight at my sides
that my fingernails would pierce my palms.

There's something in you,
that rubs people the wrong way.
Something angry,
something dark and controlling.
It doesn't come from me,
but it's there. It's always been there.
I hope for your sake you learn to control it.
Before it kills you. Before it hurts anything else.

Today a pūriri moth sat beside me.
Takata wairua, takata wairua, I sang
as it crawled onto my outstretched hand,
moving over fingers that have learnt to rest.
Takata wairua, takata wairua. Ko au ko koe, ko koe ko au.

Even the hard kōwhai seed
softens in time to produce a seedling,
the hard gold fading to soft brown.

He flies away,
I do not notice him go.
I simply notice that my hand is empty.

River Songs—Future Stream

Pāpā, you do not need to worry about me.
For last night I dreamed myself a river
with a good man crossing it.
The river was bursting with watercress,
and as clear as the ones you had taught me to drink from.

You would cup your hands
and lower them into the ripples,
watching the water surge up between your fingers.
Then slowly tighten and pull up
out of our mountain stream.
You would tilt back my infant head
and gently pour the water past my lips.
The cold cutting me down my centre
like a night in the snow.

Pāpā, the man held a little girl.
She pressed her face into his shoulder
like I used to do,
her clothes wet from drinking from that river.
Her hair lighter than any I'd seen
but her skin golden like yours, his
and mine.

He is walking towards me on the bank
as I look on him.
Family gather on the grass,
but no matter where I look
you are not there this time.
Pāpā, you do not need to worry.
I see the darkness of you
in her.

Acknowledgements

Ko tōku whānau; tōku māpihi maurea ki te ao Māori, ki te ao o ō tātou tūpuna. This book is for you, us, and all who come after us. With this I acknowledge my family in a te ao Māori sense: all the whanauka who have helped to nourish my wairua. Every time I fall, it is no longer into the dark bottomless place that can be seen in these poems, but onto the beautiful whāriki of love and compassion that you all have woven beneath me.

To my pāpā, John, my mum, Jane, and my grandfather, Noel. To Matthew Wildbore, who would have loved this book. To Walter George Koha Solly, who would have been embarrassed to have a poem about him but would secretly have loved it. To my other grandfather, George, who nourished my love of books. To my Nana Judy, who holds me closer than anyone ever has. To Grandy, Robyn Wildbore, my loudest supporter. To my partner, Daniela Butterfield, who has held my hand the entire time. To my Kāi Tahu oracle / best friend, cousin Ihāia Ryan, thanks for all your reckons. To the beautiful writers in my whānau, Arihia and Pōua Gerry, I am so proud to join our whānau legacy with this book that will sit next to Pōua's on the shelf.

To Soldiers Rd for their beautiful cover and Hinewirangi Kohu Morgan for adorning us with taoka, thank you for your manaakitaka, your aroha, and the care you took in gifting us back the family taoka that is this portrait. To Leisa Aumua: tōku whanauka, thank you for gifting the art of our tūpuna.

To Anahera, Fergus, Ashleigh and VUP, thanks for letting me hold tino rakatirataka within the publishing process. Thanks to editors at *Mimicry*, *The Spinoff*, *Starling*, and *Toi Māori*, where some of these poems first appeared.

I'm lucky to be part of an amazing community of writers including Te Hā, Te Whē and Rakatahi o te Pene. Special mentions to Tayi Tibble and essa may ranapiri, thank you for always bringing all of us with you wherever you go. Thanks to Tina Makareti, who has provided constant support. To Sinead, Freya, Claudia, Rebecca(s), Michelle, Stacey, Rahiri. Thanks to *Starling*'s Francis and Louise for bringing so many of these people together.

Special mentions to the taonga puoro whānau: Al and Ariana, Elyse, Tamihana, Sam, Ricky, Seb, Jess, Rob, Jhan, Kahu, Khali and everyone I have shared rangi with. Puoro is the real poetry, and you are all its writers.

And lastly, to all little snot-nosed Kāi Tahu girls trying to negotiate walking in two worlds. This one's for you. I wish you all the very best.

Glossary

ahi kā: home fires, people who keep the home fires burning
harakeke: flax
he manawa maunga: a mountain heart
Kei hea tōku pāpā?: Where is my father?
kōauau: Māori flute
Kōia kōia, e tau e kōia: Dig, dig, settle down and dig (from a Kāi
    Tahu mōteatea, or lament)
koukou: the sound of the ruru
mamae: hurt, pain
kā manu ika: the fish birds
kā whetū: the stars
Paikea: ancestor of Kāi Tahu
Papatūānuku: Earth Mother
porotiti: A spun instrument used during the influenza epidemic to
    help with breathing
puawhanaka: clematis (in Kāi Tahu dialect)
pūrerehua: an instrument that is swung in the air, making a
    whirring sound.
Rakinui: Sky Father (in Kāi Tahu dialect)
raruraru: problem
tāku kōtiro: my girl
Tāwhirimātea: the god of the wind
te marama: the moon
Te Pukapuka a Hoani: The Book of John
te reo o te marama: the language of the moon
Te Whare o Hoani: The House of John
wairaki: mental illness
whenua: land, placenta
Whetū Hana: Bright Star